D0847802

Big League Dreams

Also by Richard Brignall in the Lorimer Recordbooks
series:

Big Train: The legendary ironman of sport, Lionel Conacher

Fearless: The story of George Chuvalo, Canada's greatest boxer

*Forever Champions: The enduring legacy of the record-setting
    Edmonton Grads*

*Small Town Glory: The story of the Kenora Thistles' remarkable
    quest for the Stanley Cup* (with John Danakas)

Big League Dreams

Dreams

Richard Brignall

James Lorimer & Company, Ltd., Publishers
Toronto

James Lorimer & Company Ltd. acknowledges the support of the Ontario Arts Council. We acknowledge the support of the Government of Canada through the Book Publishing Industry Development Program (BPIDP) for our publishing activities. We acknowledge the support of the Canada Council for the Arts for our publishing program. We acknowledge the assistance of the OMDC Book Fund, and initiative of Ontario Media Development Corporation.

Cover design: Meredith Bangay

Library and Archives Canada Cataloguing in Publication

Brignall, Richard
    Big league dreams : Baseball Hall of Fame's first African Canadian, Fergie Jenkins / Richard Brignall.
(Recordbooks) Includes index.

ISBN 978-1-55277-487-8 (bound).—ISBN 978-1-55277-486-1 (pbk.)

    1. Jenkins, Ferguson, 1943- —Juvenile literature. 2. Black Canadian baseball players—Biography—Juvenile literature. I. Title. II. Series: Recordbooks

GV865.J38B75 2010   j796.357092   C2009-906935-0

James Lorimer & Company Ltd., Publishers
317 Adelaide Street West,
Suite #1002
Toronto, ON
M5V 1P9
www.lorimer.ca

Distributed in the U.S. by:
Orca Book Publishers
P.O. Box 468
Custer, WA USA
98240-0468

Printed and bound in Canada.

Manufactured by Webcom in Toronto, Ontario, Canada in February 2010.
Job# 366655

I dedicate this book to my wife Shelley. Every writer needs an understanding partner, especially when the deadline is fast approaching. I am lucky to have one in Shelley.

Contents

Prologue 9

1   Small-town Life 13

2   Picking Baseball 21

3   A New Position 27

4   Raw Talent 32

5   Turning Pro 39

6   Surrounded by Hate 46

7   Major-League Disappointment 57

8   A New Start 67

9   Breakout Year 76

10   A Family Tragedy 84

11   A Canadian First 93

12   A Class by Himself 103

13   Comeback 111

14   Troubled Career 117

15   Guilty? 124

16   One Last Chance 130

Epilogue 138

Glossary 142

Acknowledgements 146

About the Author *148*

Photo Credits *149*

Index *150*

Prologue

The National Baseball Hall of Fame is known as "Cooperstown." This is because it is located in the town of Cooperstown, in New York State. Baseball's best players are enshrined inside its walls. Every ballplayer dreams of one day entering as a new member.

Baseball players are eligible for induction into the Hall of Fame five years after their retirement. This is when their names are added to a list of baseball greats still trying for a spot. They must be voted in by the Baseball Writers' Association of America. To make the Hall, a candidate's name must appear on 75 per cent of the ballots cast by the writers. Many great baseball players have not been voted in.

Many thought Canadian pitcher Ferguson Jenkins had a chance of being elected to the Hall. Fergie was a top pitcher during most of his career. His statistics when he retired in 1983 were equal to or better than other Hall of Fame pitchers.

But Fergie was up against megastars in the voting. Some of them had been on winning teams. Their faces were familiar from appearing in advertisements and TV commercials.

Fergie's first year on the ballot was in 1989. He finished fifth in voting. Former Cincinnati Reds player Johnny Bench and Boston Red Sox player Carl Yastrzemski were selected instead.

On the 1990 ballot Fergie finished fourth in voting. Former Baltimore Orioles pitcher Jim Palmer and Joe Morgan of the Cincinnati Reds were selected.

Fergie was disappointed.

The evening of January 8, 1991, Fergie was at home fixing supper. The telephone rang and Fergie picked up the receiver.

"This is Jack Lang." It was the secretary of the Baseball Writers' Association of America. "Let me be the first to congratulate you on your election to the Hall of Fame."

1   Small-town Life

Baseball is America's game. It is played in every town across the country. Every child who plays dreams of becoming the next great power hitter or pitcher.

In Canada, kids dream of careers in pro sports, too. Canadians love to play hockey. Every young hockey player dreams of one day playing in the National Hockey League (NHL). But in some small towns across Canada there are young ballplayers with big-league dreams of their own.

At one time these young Canadians didn't have many homegrown baseball heroes. Instead, they looked up to American stars. That all changed when Ferguson Jenkins became a major-league pitcher. The player nicknamed Fergie became Canada's baseball superstar.

Fergie was born on December 13, 1942, in Chatham, Ontario. His family background was African-American and Caribbean. He was black in a town of mostly white people. This difference didn't make him feel out of place. He always felt like he was a part of the community. He lived alongside Japanese, Polish, Dutch, and other black people.

"We were all Canadian. There was no race discrimination," said Fergie. "We were all the same. Nobody cared if you were black or not."

Almost everyone who lived in Chatham loved hockey. When he was about five years old Fergie's father bought him his first pair of skates. He was playing in a league by age seven.

Fergie's father was his first major influence in sports. His name was also Ferguson. The senior Ferguson Jenkins was a ballplayer before Fergie was born. He played semi-pro baseball from 1925 to the early 1940s. He wasn't allowed to play major-league baseball because of the colour of his skin. He played in the Negro Leagues and various Ontario-based leagues.

Ferguson senior wanted to pass his love for baseball on to his son. As soon as Fergie was old enough, father and son would spend hours at the local park playing baseball. Fergie's love of baseball became linked with his love for his father.

Baseball had even brought Fergie's parents together. His father came to Chatham to play on a baseball team. He eventually stayed because of his wife, Fergie's mother, Delores.

Delores was descended from runaway slaves who had come to the Chatham area via the Underground Railroad. The Underground Railroad was not like any railroad today. It was a network of people, secret routes, and safe houses — not tracks. It was put in place to help black slaves escape the United States. Between thirty and one hundred thousand black slaves used it to escape to Canada and freedom, the majority between 1850 and 1860.

Fergie's mother Delores lost her sight during the birth of her son. She was blind for the rest of her life. But she never showed regret about the price she had paid.

"My mother might have been my biggest fan, but it was not because she was a baseball fan," said Fergie. "She was a fan of me."

Fergie played every sport he could while he was growing up. He excelled at

Delores Jenkins holds her baby boy Ferguson Jenkins Jr. He became the greatest joy in her life.

*The Kansas City Monarchs and the Hilldale baseball
teams line up before the 1924 Negro League World Series.*

baseball, hockey, basketball, and track and
field. His skin colour never kept him from
playing any sport. But his father knew it
wasn't like that everywhere.

In just about every pro sport, the colour
barrier kept black players out of the major
leagues. There were black leagues and
white leagues. Generations of black and
white pro athletes were forced to play
apart. But that would all change. Fergie
would be able to live his life differently. It
was all because of one black ballplayer.
His name was Jackie Robinson.

On April 18, 1947, Jackie Robinson played baseball for the Brooklyn Dodgers of the National League. He was the first black player in the history of major-league baseball. He brought down the colour barrier for all black athletes. Baseball would never be the same. The colour barrier in other sports would fall over the next decade.

Unfortunately, it happened too late for Fergie's father to live out his dream. He was too old to play major-league baseball. But his son had the chance to play pro baseball. Fergie's future would be determined by his skills, not by the colour of his skin.

Breaking the Colour Barrier

Starting in the 1880s, black baseball players formed their own teams and leagues. These leagues were generally called the Negro Leagues. Cool Papa Bell, Satchel Paige, and Josh Gibson were the stars. Jackie Robinson started his professional baseball career with the Kansas City Monarchs of the Negro Leagues. In 1945 he was signed to the Brooklyn Dodgers. Before his major-league debut in 1947, Jackie played for the Dodgers' minor-league team, the Montreal Royals. Robinson won the Rookie-of-the-Year award, and two years later was named National League Most Valuable Player. During his career he played in six World Series championships and six consecutive All-Star Games. He retired from baseball in 1956. But it wasn't until 1958 that the Negro Leagues played their last game.

2 Picking Baseball

When Fergie was growing up in Chatham, he went from one sport to another. As the season changed, so did the sport Fergie and his friends were playing. When Fergie was eight or nine he started playing in a baseball league. Then, he was just an average kid playing baseball. "I was struggling like everybody else," said Fergie.

His sporting life started to change when he was twelve. That was when his body started to mature. He grew long and lean and became a better athlete. He started to focus on becoming a better baseball player.

As a teenager, Fergie was very tall for his age, so his coaches put him on first base. His father bought him a first-baseman's glove. Fergie learned that if he played this position well, his team had a better chance of winning the game.

"Turning fourteen was kind of a watershed year for me. That's when I first started to think about playing sports professionally," said Fergie. "It wasn't because I was such a great athlete, but the idea sprung from going to my first NHL game and my first major-league baseball game. What I saw provided inspiration."

Fergie went to see an exhibition game between the Toronto Maple Leafs and the Boston Bruins. One of the players on the Bruins was Willie O'Ree. O'Ree was the first black player in the history of the NHL. He was proving a black man could

Chatham is a small town in southwestern Ontario, near London. Here's what the downtown looked like when Fergie was growing up there.

make it to the highest level.

"Seeing Willie O'Ree play in the NHL at the time when there were only six teams made me think," said Fergie. "I thought that was going to be my ticket."

At one time Fergie played more hockey

than any other sport. His goal was to play junior hockey with the Chatham Maroons. Inspired by O'Ree, he also wanted to play in the NHL. When that didn't work out, it didn't stop him dreaming about playing pro sports.

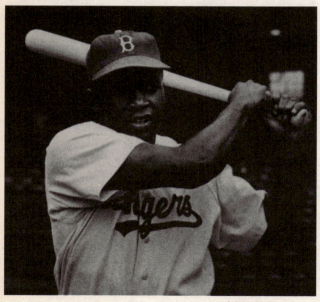

Jackie Robinson was a great athlete who played many sports in college. It was in baseball that he became a legend.

Jackie Robinson of Hockey

Willie O'Ree was from New Brunswick. On January 18, 1958, he played for the Boston Bruins against the Montreal Canadiens. That made him the first black man to play in the NHL. His pro hockey career lasted twenty years.

Fergie went to his first major-league baseball game when he was fourteen. The Detroit Tigers were playing the Cleveland Indians. One of the notable players on the Indians was Larry Doby, a black player.

It was widely known that Jackie Robinson broke the colour barrier in major-league baseball in 1947. But not everybody remembered Larry Doby's feat. A few months after Robinson's first game, Doby joined the Indians. He broke the colour barrier in the American League.

"In the game I saw with my dad, Larry

Doby hit two homeruns. I was struck by how the fans cheered him. That was the first time I had seen a player from a visiting ball club get cheered by the Detroit Tigers fans," said Fergie. "That made a big impression on me. I told my father, 'You know, Dad, I think I want to play baseball.'"

Fergie didn't stop playing other sports. He still played hockey in the winter. At school he was on the basketball and track-and-field teams. But now had a focus — on becoming a better baseball player, to be the best first baseman he could be. It was as a baseball player, like Larry Doby, where he could turn pro some day.

3 A New Position

All baseball players know how to throw a ball. It is an important part of the game. This does not mean all players can pitch. That takes special talent. A pitcher must be able to throw the ball over the narrow home plate. A pitcher must make sure the batter does not get a hit. This means a pitcher must throw the ball with accuracy and speed.

Fergie was not seen as a pitcher. He was always the team's first baseman. His height gave him an advantage at that position. He could reach out and nab balls better than any shorter player could. But, unknown to other people, he wanted to try pitching. He wanted to see if he could do it, even if it was just for one game.

As a young player, Fergie had honed his skills as a pitcher without knowing it. Terry's Coal Yard was located across the street from his home. Fergie and his friends used to pick up pieces of coal and throw them at the building. They tried to get the coal through an opening in the building.

Then Fergie and his friends took aim at passing train boxcars. They did not want to hit them. They wanted to time their throws so the rocks would pass between the cars.

"I tried to throw the rocks between the narrowest spaces separating the moving boxcars," said Fergie.

This off-field training came in handy

when Fergie was playing for the Chatham Junior Baseball All Star team.

His team only had two pitchers, Jack Howe and Mark Cundle. They ran into a problem when two games were scheduled on one weekend. Cundle pitched on the Saturday. Howe was set to pitch Sunday, but he turned up with a sore arm. He could hardly throw the ball to the plate.

It was too much to expect Cundle to pitch two nights in a row. Coach Doug Allen didn't want to risk injuring Cundle's arm. He called the team together.

"All right," said Coach Allen. "We've got a problem and it's up to you to solve it. I cannot ask Mark to pitch again and I don't want to force anyone to pitch against their will. Who's going to volunteer?"

Nobody seemed eager to pitch. Fergie saw his chance to try the position. With no players stepping forward, why not him?

"I'll do it, Coach," Fergie said. "I'll start

if you want me to. I think I can do it. Me, Fergie Jenkins."

Coach Allen scratched his head, but finally he said, "Well, go ahead. I know you can throw hard. Anyway, we don't have much of a choice."

The other coaches agreed it was the only thing to do.

"I felt awkward and uncomfortable," said Fergie about the first game he pitched. "All I knew about pitching was that I had to throw the ball hard and get it over the plate."

Fergie's first game as a pitcher opened everyone's eyes. He pitched an amazing game. Over seven innings, he struck out fifteen batters and gave up only two hits.

For the rest of the season Fergie was a starting pitcher for his team. When he wasn't pitching, he still played first base. He was a success at both positions. But he knew he still had a lot to learn as a pitcher.

Studying the Foe

A pitcher must know what type of hitter they are pitching against. They need to know what types of pitches the batter likes to hit. They need to know what pitches give them trouble. Fergie became a smart pitcher after he hit the majors. He kept a book that described each player's strengths and weaknesses. He studied it before every game he pitched in.

4 Raw Talent

The baseball season in Ontario was short, only fifteen to twenty-five games. Fergie pitched seven or eight games, and played first base for the rest. He wanted to focus on baseball and become a pitcher but couldn't do it on his own. Luckily, he found a mentor who could help him with his game.

"Being the pitcher meant you were a little bit more active than just standing at first base waiting for something to happen," said Fergie. "It provided the feeling of being more part of the game."

Gene Dzadura was always on the lookout for good baseball players. He had been a pro baseball player. After his ball career ended he became a teacher in Windsor, Ontario. He was also a scout for the Philadelphia Phillies, a major-league baseball team.

In 1959, one of the teachers at Chatham Vocational School needed a teacher to sub for him when he was away getting married. Gene answered his call. To pique his interest he had been told about a couple of promising young players.

Gene drove up from Windsor to Chatham. He asked Fergie to meet him at the high school. Fergie pitched to Gene. Gene put him through a tough workout.

"It was a weekday in the winter. Nobody was around. He watched me throw in the gymnasium," said Fergie. "At fifteen, I was really raw and crude."

Gene thought Fergie showed potential for a future as a pitcher. Maybe even as a pro pitcher. Sure there were some rough edges, but they could be corrected with a little training.

Fergie became Gene's student.

"Fergie was very coachable," said Gene. "He listened to what I told him. And he was dedicated. He never missed a workout, even if it meant he had to miss a date or some other event."

Over the next three years, Gene taught Fergie every aspect of the game. In summer they trained at local ballparks. In winter Fergie pitched to Gene in the school gym.

Fergie's pitching improved. He started to think he might have a chance at becoming a pro pitcher. Gene thought so, too.

"Gene encouraged me to work hard so that I could become a major-league pitcher. He was constantly prodding me on and showing me how to improve myself," said Fergie. He would have to match the skill and training of the players he would meet in pro play in the United States. "Almost everything I did at this time was dedicated toward preparing me mentally and physically for a professional baseball career."

When Fergie wasn't practising his pitching, he would beg his father to drive him to Detroit. The American city was only ninety kilometres from Chatham. Both Ferguson Jenkinses would go to watch Detroit Tigers baseball games.

"I used to see Jim Bunning of the Tigers pitch and I wondered if the day would ever come if I would ever meet him or any other big-leaguer," said Fergie.

Fergie watched and dreamed about becoming a big-league baseball player. His father wanted him to make his dreams come true. He gave Fergie advice to help guide him to that goal.

"We talked about the time required to become a baseball player. I realized at this time that dreams take hard work. He told me there are thousands of other high-school kids like me who are in the stands and want the same dream. Therefore I had to work hard," said Fergie.

As Fergie's skills improved, he came to the attention of Tony Lucadello, chief scout for the Philadelphia Phillies. Tony became another mentor for Fergie. He taught Fergie how to throw different pitches better. He showed him how to grip the ball harder to increase the speed of his fastball. He taught him how to increase the rotation of the curveball so it would break better.

Other scouts from major-league organizations came to Chatham to see Fergie. They saw him as a first baseman or an outfielder. But Fergie thought of himself as a pitcher.

The Phillies organization saw Fergie as a promising pitcher, too. Their scouts, Gene and Tony, became friends to Fergie's family. Fergie's parents were determined that he sign with the Phillies and no one else.

Fergie graduated from Chatham Vocational High School in June of 1962. He was eighteen years old. A couple of days later, he signed a pro contract with the Philadelphia Phillies.

"Gene and Tony did not just scout me — they educated me in baseball. They invested three years in me before I ever signed with the Phillies," said Fergie.

Fergie received a $7,500 signing bonus and a salary of $400 a month. He gave his signing bonus to his mother and father to pay off the mortgage on their home.

"It was a small repayment for all the

love and care and understanding they had invested in me," said Fergie. "This is something no amount of money could ever buy."

Fergie could hardly wait to leave home and start his pro baseball career.

5 Turning Pro

Fergie had worked hard to get scouted and signed by the Phillies. Now he had to work even harder to earn a spot on the Phillies major-league roster. He started his pro baseball career in the Phillies minor-league system. He had to work his way up their minor-league system like every other player. He had to develop his skills as a pitcher. If he didn't, he would never be a major-league pitcher.

Right after signing his contract, Fergie

was assigned to a team in Williamsport, Pennsylvania. It was a Class A team in the Phillies farm system.

Fergie's parents drove him to Detroit so he could fly to his first baseball assignment. It would be his first time on an airplane. His dad had to comfort his

Major and Minor Leagues

The minor leagues are not a single league. They are different leagues based in different regions across North America. Each league is classed by the players' skill level. It is how players are trained to become major-league players. In the minors, they "grow" into better ballplayers. This is why the minor leagues are also called the farm system. Class A leagues are the lowest level in the minors. It is where all rookies start. Class AAA leagues are the highest. It is where the best players go before joining a major-league team. Not all players who start in Class A make it up to Class AAA.

mother. She was sad to see her son go. This was an important moment for Fergie. He was leaving home for the first time. He was entering a world that might not be like Chatham.

"This is the life he wants, and we'll just have to let him go on his own," Fergie's dad told his mom. "He has a great opportunity and we should be thankful that he's getting this chance."

Fergie had a hard time leaving his mother, though. "I always felt kind of guilty leaving her, but I knew I had to pursue my career," he said.

Fergie's mother gave him lots of advice while he was growing up. He remembered one piece of advice she gave to help him through leaving them that day: "If you're trying to do something, do the best you can. Whatever you start, finish."

Fergie was ready to start his career. He was ready to work hard not to fail.

Fergie arrived in Williamsport while the team was on the road. He settled down at the Williamsport Hotel. He would share the room with one of his new teammates. That new teammate was shocked to see that Fergie was black.

"In 1962, white and black athletes did not room together," said Fergie.

Fergie was not the only black player on the team. The black players shared an apartment. Fergie had to move in with them.

This was the first time Fergie saw that being black in Chatham was different from being black in other places.

"Chatham was a virtually prejudice-free environment," said Fergie. "I was aware of being black, but I never dwelled on it. I just was black, like my other friends were white."

It was one small thing, and Fergie didn't let it worry him. He was eighteen years old and wanted to play baseball. But he

This photo taken in the late 1930 in the southern United States shows a boy at a segregated water fountain. Things were different for Fergie's family in Canada than for blacks in the United States.

realized things might be different from that point on.

In Williamsport, Fergie didn't see any game action. The team's manager, Frank Lucchesi, didn't know what to do with him. The Phillies didn't know either. He was a raw talent with potential. They wanted Fergie to get used to the pro baseball experience.

The highlight for Fergie was getting into his uniform and throwing batting practice before each game. Once the game started, he was in his own clothes sitting in the stands. He did not complain about not playing. He wanted to make a good first impression, and knew he was just an unknown pitching prospect from Canada.

Manager Lucchesi kept an eye on Fergie to see what type of person he was. He watched Fergie's work habits and how he pitched. The Phillies were wondering where to send him next.

One day Lucchesi pulled Fergie aside for a talk.

"Fergie, you've shown me that you want to earn a living at the game," said Lucchesi. "I like the way you've been working and the attitude you've shown."

Fergie was sent to pitch in Miami, Florida. He would join the Miami Marlins, a Class A team in the Phillies farm system.

6 Surrounded by Hate

In Miami, Fergie finally got to pitch in a pro baseball game. But along with it came an experience he didn't expect. He quickly discovered what it meant to be a black man in the southern United States.

"As a Canadian I had no real concept of bigotry and segregation. I had read about the South in the newspaper and had seen scenes of violence and protest marches on television, but now for the first time I was part of it," said Fergie.

He was refused service at restaurants along with the other black players. They also could not room in the same hotels as white players.

"As a child in Chatham I knew the pigmentation of my skin was dark, but this realization that 'black' meant 'different' did not come to me until after I signed to play baseball professionally," said Fergie. "All these things grated on me, but they did not make me angry. I just felt sorry for the narrow-mindedness of the people who could do such things."

It was 1962, and it was a time for change in the United States. The civil rights movement was rising up in the American South. Rights activists wanted things to change for the better for black people. But many of the white people in the South were not ready yet.

At one point, Fergie witnessed a form of hate he thought he would never see,

Civil rights marches, like the one shown here, were held to demand equal rights for blacks.

and he would never forget it. A peaceful protest by twenty black youths was broken up in a park by white youths. They became physically violent and tossed rotten food and eggs at the protesters.

"I saw things in Miami involving human relations like that, that I would have been happy never to have seen," said Fergie. But he knew that, to get through it, he had to focus his efforts.

"I wasn't there to be a crusader or a politician," he explained. "I was just a teenager. I was there to play baseball. That's what I had to focus on."

In Miami, Fergie didn't just learn about the ugly side of life. In the clubhouse, he got some important advice from Miami Marlins manager Paul Seminuk.

"If you are going to succeed, have pride in yourself," said Seminuk. "Prove to yourself that you belong in a Miami Marlins uniform or whatever uniform you will be wearing later on. If you don't believe that you belong, nobody else is going to believe it either."

Fergie stayed with the Marlins for only

a month. He impressed the Phillies by striking out 69 batters in 65 innings. He was promoted to a higher league. He finished the 1962 season in Buffalo, New York, on a Class AAA team. He was playing at the highest minor-league level. All the other players were older and Fergie felt a little out of place.

Fergie attended his first major-league training camp in the spring of 1963. All the players in the Phillies organization were looked at before the season started. Some players were good enough to stay with the major-league club. Others were sent down to the minors for more development.

The Phillies were satisfied with the progress Fergie had made in 1962. He signed a new contract that paid him $800 a month. He started the 1963 regular season in Little Rock, Arkansas. He would pitch for the Arkansas Travelers of the

Class AAA Pacific Coast League.

Fergie was part of the first group of black players to play in Little Rock. The other players included Richie Allen, Dick Quiroz, Frank Barnes, and Marcelino Lopez.

"There was discrimination in Miami and I learned to adjust to it, but things were tenser in Arkansas," said Fergie.

When the team arrived in Little Rock, there was a crowd of people waiting for them. They held signs saying they didn't want black players on the team. In the locker room, the team had kept the sign on the wall that read: "No black ballplayers on the team."

The locker room was separated into two parts. The black players had their own section for their lockers, washrooms, and water fountains. It was like that in the rest of the ballpark, too. The black fans could only sit down the right field line. They mainly cheered for the new black players.

Little Rock was a deep concern for Fergie's mother. She knew that, as a Canadian, he had not suffered from the treatment that American blacks endured. In Chatham there was no segregation. There were no separate washrooms, drinking fountains, or sections at ballparks.

In Little Rock, the black players were not allowed to eat or drink with their white teammates. Many times, waitresses wouldn't serve them at restaurants. White-skinned players stayed at good hotels in every city. Their black teammates were sent to motels in the black areas of town.

The black players on the team were the focus of racial abuse from white people in the stands. Racist fans would call out names at them. One time they covered Richie Allen's car with hurtful signs and scrawls on the windows. What surprised Fergie was that the messages on the car

A Segregated Hall of Fame

The first group of players elected into the Baseball Hall of Fame in 1936 had two things in common. First, they were all the greatest players of their time. Second, not one of them had played pro baseball alongside a black man. The first inductees included Ty Cobb, Babe Ruth, Honus Wagner, Christy Mathewson, and Walter Johnson. The first black player elected to the Hall of Fame was Jackie Robinson in 1962. In 1971 the Hall of Fame started to elect the stars of the Negro Leagues.

and shouts from the stands were from fans of their team.

"They didn't want us there in the first place and I wasn't there to fight," said Fergie. "I was there to play baseball. I didn't let it bother me."

"As Martin Luther King, Jr., said, I always kept my eyes on the prize," said

Fergie. "I figured I could put up with these inconveniences if I treated them only as inconveniences and didn't let them poison my attitude or distract me from my business."

Teammate Richie Allen was affected the most when he came to Little Rock. This was the first time he was exposed to real racism. It hurt him greatly. It changed him as a person and made him moody and angry. He dreamed of the day the Phillies would get him out of Little Rock.

"Allen was an everyday player, so they were on him all the time," said Fergie. "Marcelino Lopez and I just pitched every couple of days and they didn't bother us as much."

Fergie didn't pitch much at Little Rock. He wasn't ready to pitch at such a high level. After only a few weeks, he was sent back down to the Class A team in Miami. He became one of the best pitchers the

Marlins had. He had a 12–5 record when the season ended.

During the 1964 season, Fergie continued his climb up the Phillies farm system. He started the season playing for the Class AA Chattanooga Lookouts. It was when he was playing with the Lookouts that Fergie's parents first got to watch their son play pro baseball.

After pitching ten wins in a row with the Chattanooga Lookouts, Fergie was sent back up to Class AAA in Little Rock.

A Pitcher's Record

The main statistic for every pitcher is their win-loss record. The win-loss record is the number of wins and losses a pitcher has in his career or a single season. A pitcher's total wins and losses are commonly put together. An example of a pitcher's record might be 12-10, which says that pitcher has 12 wins and 10 losses.

He would once again pitch for the Arkansas Travelers. This time he was ready to pitch at the higher level.

When Fergie returned to Little Rock, he thought he would be surrounded by hate. But there was a change. He found that he was slowly being accepted by the Travelers fans. By the end of the 1964 season, those fans surprised him and voted him as the most popular player.

7 Major-League Disappointment

Fergie had all the usual reasons for wanting to be a big-league pitcher. He would have fame and money. But the most powerful reason was back in his hometown of Chatham.

Ferguson senior never knew if he could have made it as a big-leaguer. His own hopes and dreams were wrapped up in his son. The name Ferguson Jenkins in a Philadelphia box score would represent the dreams of two men.

After a successful 1964 season in the minors, Fergie hoped he would be chosen as a starting pitcher for the Phillies. But the Phillies had other plans for him. They decided he should concentrate on becoming a relief pitcher.

As a relief pitcher, Fergie would come into the game to replace the starting pitcher. When the starting pitcher is hurt or tired, or isn't pitching well, it is up to the relief pitcher to save the game.

"It made no difference to me whether I was to start or pitch in relief," said Fergie, who at that point just wanted to be a major-league pitcher.

During 1965 spring training, the Phillies were counting on two veteran pitchers to do most of the relief work. There was at least one spot on the roster for another relief pitcher. Fergie thought he had shown the Phillies he could do it.

Before the end of spring training, Fergie

was called into the office of Phillies manager Gene Mauch. He sat down with the manager and expected to hear that he had made the roster.

"Jenkins, I appreciate how hard you have been working," Mauch said, "and we think you've made some progress. But we think you need more work, more experience, that you would not get with us. We're going to send you to Little Rock, but I'm sure you'll be back before the season is over."

Fergie was shocked to be going back to the minors. But he had to follow the Phillies' orders. He remembered the early advice of Manager Seminuk to work hard no matter what uniform he was in. He would have to, if he ever wanted to pitch in the major leagues.

Fergie went back to Little Rock to show the Phillies he should be in the majors. He had a good season with Little

Rock and an 8–6 record. He impressed the right people without knowing it.

"What I like about Fergie is that he throws strikes," said Cal McLish, the Phillies pitching coach. "Some scouts told me they didn't like his fastball. So I went down to Dallas one night and watched him work. He threw fifty-two fastballs before one was hit out of the infield. I decided I liked him."

By September, Mauch decided he wanted Fergie with the Phillies. Fergie was at last in a Phillies uniform.

Fergie pitched his first game in the major leagues on September 6, 1965, against the St. Louis Cardinals. He was only twenty-one years old. His parents could not come to watch the game. Instead, they listened to it on the radio.

The Phillies starting pitcher was Jim Bunning. He was one of the pitchers Fergie had admired while he was growing up. Fergie had dreamed of the day when they would be teammates. He could ask Bunning many questions about pitching.

Bunning had pitched eight innings when Fergie was called to relieve him. Bunning had allowed men to reach first and third. The score was tied. Manager Mauch strutted out to the mound.

"I'm taking you out," Mauch told an upset Bunning.

After handing Mauch the ball, an angry Bunning headed for the dugout. He glanced back to see who was relieving him. Then he stopped short of the dugout steps. He did not like what he saw.

"Are you serious?" Bunning yelled at Mauch. "Him?!" He pointed at Fergie.

Bunning didn't like the fact that he was being replaced by a rookie.

Fergie took his warm-up pitches when he reached the mound. Once he was set, he nervously stared at the catcher. The catcher always tells the pitcher what pitch to throw. Fergie was waiting for the sign. After checking the base runners, he threw the first pitch of his major-league career.

The pitch went straight at the batter's head. The batter fell to the ground as it flew past his ear. As he fell, the ball hit his bat. This foul ball was Fergie's first major-league strike. The next two pitches were also strikes. Fergie had his first strikeout. By the end of the game, he had pitched four innings of relief and the Phillies won 5–4.

Back in Chatham, his parents were excited to watch their son's pro career unfold. Even though they never went to any games, they followed them closely. His mother listened to the stories her husband read from *The Sporting News* and Philadelphia newspapers. Afterwards she sat and typed out letters of encouragement to her son.

8 A New Start

When Fergie joined the Chicago Cubs, he wanted to prove to them he belonged. He didn't want to be traded again. But his future wasn't secure with the Cubs. He was an afterthought in the trade. Cubs manager Leo Durocher was really after speedy outfielder Adolfo Phillips.

"Leo Durocher couldn't have known what he was getting when he got Ferguson Jenkins," said Atlanta Braves manager Luman Harris.

Most of the attention that season was given to pitcher Kenny Holtzman. They said he was the league's next great pitcher. In his shadow, Fergie's career would rise.

Fergie sat in the bullpen in his first game with the Chicago Cubs. A day later, on April 23, 1966, he got his chance to pitch for his new club.

It was in a game against the Los Angeles Dodgers. The Cubs starting pitcher struggled. At the beginning of the third inning, Leo Durocher pulled the starting pitcher. He left the game with the bases loaded and two out. The manager signalled to the bullpen that he wanted a relief pitcher. Fergie ran out from the bullpen to the mound. John Kennedy was at bat. Kennedy flied out to end the inning. Fergie had got the Cubs out of their jam.

Fergie made a great first impression on the Chicago fans after that inning. While at bat he hit his first major-league homerun.

Pitcher at Plate

Pitchers are usually the weakest hitters on a team. In the National League, the pitcher has to take their turn in the batting order and go to bat. It is different in the American League. To make the game more exciting, a designated hitter replaces the pitcher in the batting order. Fergie was a good hitting pitcher. In his major league career he had 148 hits, 13 homeruns, and 85 runs-batted-in (RBIs). His best year was in 1971, when he hit 6 homeruns and had 20 RBIs.

That gave the Cubs a 1–0 lead. Later in the game, he singled home another run. The Cubs were leading 2–0.

On the mound Fergie was equally good. He did not allow the Dodgers to score a single run. He allowed only four hits in the five innings he pitched. He got his first win as a Cub with a 2–0 final score.

Wrigley Field is home to the Chicago Cubs. The team was known as "the lovable losers" of Major League Baseball because they hadn't won a World Series since 1908.

"The legend of Ferguson Arthur Jenkins started in the damp chill of Wrigley Field yesterday," wrote Richard Dozier of the *Chicago Tribune*. "6,974 fans can always tell their grandchildren, 'I was there on the day Jenkins first pitched for the Cubs.'"

The Cubs had started the 1966 season with a 1–8 win–loss record. They were at the bottom of the National League standings all season. By the beginning of

May their poor play continued. They could only muster a 4–15 record.

Fans of the team were looking for anything positive to say about the club. One of the only bright spots was the pitching of Fergie Jenkins. He was called on to pitch more than any other pitcher on the team. With all that work, he thought he was going to make a career as a relief pitcher.

Manager Durocher was looking for ways to get his team out of the National League basement. He would do anything to win. His first plan was to experiment with Fergie.

"Durocher saw this tall, lanky guy, and Fergie showed Leo something that made him think he would be a good starting pitcher for us," said Cubs outfielder Billy Williams.

"I asked him what he wanted to be — a starter or reliever — and he said he wanted to relief. I took that for a couple of months then one day I handed him the ball and said, 'You're too good to waste yourself on that. Fergie, now you're a starter,'" said Durocher.

Durocher gave Fergie a chance to start a game against the Atlanta Braves on May 21. Fergie lasted five innings and gave up five runs. People said he didn't have what it took to be a starting pitcher. He went back to relief pitching on May 22. He struck out the last two men in the ninth inning to save a 4–3 victory for the Cubs.

Fergie was given another chance on May 29. He improved with this start. He pitched eight innings and struck out ten batters. He didn't get the win, but Durocher was impressed.

Fergie's career changed for good one day in late July. That day Durocher came to Fergie with a request.

"Fergie, we're going to start you in three days," Durocher said. "We're short of starting pitchers and you can help the club this way."

"Why me?" Fergie asked, remembering his first two times as a starter. "I'm happy to stay in the bullpen."

"No, I'm going to start you on Saturday against New York," Durocher said. "You've pitched well for us in relief and you've shown me you can go more than three or four innings."

Fergie started against the New York Mets on July 30. He pitched eight innings of good baseball. Durocher took him out with the score tied 3–3. In that game

Fergie proved to himself that he could be a starter.

He would have three starts in August and early September. Fergie still didn't have a win as a starter. But the Cubs as a whole didn't win much either. By mid August they had the worst win–loss record in the league at 43–81.

Fergie's fourth regular start since July was against the Phillies. He had pitched against his former team before, but as a reliever. He was now a starter looking for the best way to get back at the team that traded him. He did it by pitching the best game of his early career. He gave up only three hits and struck out nine to get his first victory as a starter.

"We've found another starting pitcher," Durocher said. "Fergie's beautiful."

Fergie started nine games in the second half of the season. He won four and lost two. In the other three games, he was not a part of the final decision. His season record was 6–8. The Cubs ended the season with 59 wins and 103 losses.

The people of Chatham celebrated when Fergie returned home that fall. They were proud of the local boy turned major-league pitcher. The town mayor declared October 2, 1966, to be Ferguson Jenkins Day. The people in Chatham did their best to welcome him home. Fergie appreciated what they did for him.

"When people tell you that you're doing something for Chatham and they're really pulling for you at home, it makes you try a little harder," said Fergie. "I always knew Chatham was proud of me, but these events recognizing my breaking through in the majors were pretty special."

9 Breakout Year

Manager Leo Durocher had a plan to rebuild the Cubs in 1967. He wanted to win the World Series. At the centre of that plan was Fergie. At twenty-four years of age, Fergie was looked upon to do great things. He knew he was ready for the big time. This could be the year he would prove it once and for all.

At the end of spring training, Fergie got a happy shock. Durocher named him the 1967 opening-day pitcher against the

Phillies. This was an honour given to the best pitcher on the team. Durocher thought that label now applied to Fergie.

"I was shook up when Manager Leo Durocher told me Sunday I would pitch opening day on Tuesday," said Fergie. "Boy, I sat up watching television Monday night until 1:00 a.m. to keep my mind off pitching."

Fergie had turned himself around by the next day. He was focused and serious before the game. But that calm was almost broken when he stepped out onto the field.

"I was caught off-guard that day when I heard my name called from the stands and looked up to see my parents," said Fergie. "I was pretty surprised. I had just enough time to run over and hold my mother's hand and shake hands with my dad. But I didn't have time to socialize."

Sportswriter Ernie Miller from the *London Free Press* had brought Fergie's parents down from Canada to surprise him. He wanted them to become part of his big day. It was the first time they saw him pitch in the major leagues. Because Fergie's mother was blind, she had been given a radio so she could listen to the game's play-by-play.

Fergie was nervous pitching in the first inning. It showed because he pitched poorly. In the second inning he allowed three hits. He continued to pitch poorly in the third and was almost pulled out of the game. Fortunately, no runs were scored against him. Durocher kept him in the game. In the fourth inning, Fergie finally started to pitch like the ace Durocher thought he could be.

The atmosphere of the crowd thrilled Fergie's mother. She couldn't control the tears that trickled from her sightless eyes. She was proud of her son. Inning after inning, as the crowd cheered Fergie's shutout pitching, her tears continued to flow. At different points in the game Fergie could hear her yelling out, "C'mon, baby. C'mon, Fergie."

Fergie didn't disappoint his team or his parents. He pitched a complete game. He allowed only six hits in the 4–2 victory.

The season wasn't a month old and Chicago sportswriters said Fergie was, "the man of the future," and "one of the Cubs' great ones."

By June 28, Fergie had his tenth victory of the season. He was the team's ace pitcher. The team as a whole was also playing well. The Cubs were in second place in the National League. They were only two-and-a-half games behind the first-place St. Louis Cardinals. For a couple of games the Cubs even sat on top of the league standings. That didn't last long, though. They battled for second place for the rest of the season.

Fergie was named to the National League All Star team. It was a great honour — young players rarely made the team. By the time Fergie went to the 1967 All Star Game he had an 11–5 record. It was the best record in the National League.

Fergie was the first Canadian-born pitcher to be selected as an All Star. At the game, he played alongside some of the greatest baseball players of all time. He was nervous about pitching against these legends. To get through it, all he thought about was throwing strikes.

San Francisco Giants pitcher Juan Marichal opened the game for the National League. Fergie relieved him in the third inning, and pitched three innings during the game. He struck out six batters in that time. This performance tied an All Star Game strikeout record.

One of his strikeouts was against legendary New York Yankees slugger

Mickey Mantle. The crowd gave Mantle a roaring standing ovation when he stepped up to plate. This awed Fergie. Mantle was known as one of the most powerful hitters the game had ever known. Fergie's All Star manager paid him a brief visit at the pitching mound to give him some advice. He told Fergie not to throw any soft stuff to the slugger.

"I threw Mantle two fastballs right down the pipe and he swung through the ball. It really surprised me to see him miss them," said Fergie. "The third strike just caught the corner of the plate. Mantle just watched it go by. It was a good pitch."

On September 15, 1967, Fergie broke the Cubs single-season strikeout record. The record had stood for more than fifty years. Two strikeouts in a 7–1 victory gave him 206 strikeouts for the season. This also brought his overall win–loss record to 18–12.

One of the greatest milestones for a

pitcher is a twenty-win season. Only a few pitchers achieve that record regularly. Most never come close to that kind of season.

Fergie recorded his twentieth victory on September 30. It was not something people had expected of Fergie. He impressed everybody in the league with his pitching.

He was the first twenty-game winner on the Cubs staff in three years. He led the National League with twenty complete games pitched. He also set the Cubs all-time single-season strikeout record with 236. He was second in the voting for the Cy Young Award for best pitcher.

Fergie's 1967 breakout season was not a fluke. He followed it with two more twenty-win seasons. He had a 22–16 record in 1968, and a 20–14 record in 1969. He had become one of the best pitchers in the league. Canada now had a baseball star to cheer for.

Basketball Star

In the winter of 1967, Fergie was signed to play basketball with the legendary Harlem Globetrotters. Fergie had loved playing basketball in high school back in Chatham. He was his school's star player. The Harlem Globetrotters were a travelling all-black all-star basketball team. That winter the Globetrotters played exhibition games across Canada. They thought Fergie, as a Canadian, would be a good draw for fans. Fergie played twenty games with the team that winter. He was such a good player they asked him to play for the team again in 1968. That year he appeared in eighty-five games across North America.

10 A Family Tragedy

During 1970 spring training, Fergie got an important phone call from Chatham. His mother was sick and had to be taken to the hospital. The person who called said not to worry, because she was doing fine.

Delores Jenkins had been diagnosed with cancer in 1968. Since then, her health had been failing. She was regularly in the hospital. She had lost weight and become weak, but was still fighting the disease. Fergie had driven or flown home as much

as he could to see her. This was a hard time for Fergie. He was watching his mother slowly die.

On that spring day in 1970, Fergie called his mother's doctor in Chatham. The news was not as positive as he had first heard. They had to operate. The doctor said she didn't have long to live. She had been suffering from cancer of the stomach, which had spread to her lungs and spleen.

This was terrible news for Fergie, and came at a bad time. It was before the season opener. It took his mind off baseball.

"I could not concentrate," said Fergie. "And you cannot win in baseball unless you are concentrating."

The Cubs opened the 1970 season strong. They won twelve of their first fifteen games. This included an eleven-game winning streak.

By the end of April, the Cubs were leading the National League with a 13–4 record. The season began to look promising to Cubs fans. But Fergie was not doing as well. By May 10, he had a lowly 2–5 record. It got even worse for Fergie as he continued to pitch into May.

"The Cubs were doing well in April and May, but I was not," said Fergie. "I lost seven of my first ten decisions and people were saying, 'Well this time he won't win twenty games.' It looked doubtful to me too."

Cubs pitching coach Joe Becker was Fergie's worst critic. He said that the star pitcher was not challenging batters in clutch situations.

Coach Becker saw that Fergie tended to relax against poor hitters. Becker pointed out that Fergie was getting the top hitters by throwing his best stuff. Then he tossed easy pitches that were creamed by the batters at the bottom end of the batting order. These were batters he should have easily gotten out.

Becker called Fergie in to look at some recordings of his games. Viewing them made Fergie realize what he had been doing wrong. His baseball life began to improve. With Coach Becker, he got through his problems on the field. He became the dominant pitcher he could be.

"I started to feel like a major-league pitcher again," said Fergie.

The Cubs started to climb the standings as Fergie won more games. By the end of August, Fergie had seventeen victories. It looked like another twenty-win season. On September 3, Fergie pitched his team within a half-game of the league leader. They beat the Phillies 7–2. Fergie was at the top of his game. The Phillies could only get four hits against him. But, by mid-September, baseball was once again not on Fergie's mind. After a game he got a phone call from his father in Chatham.

"Ferguson, you're going to lose your mother. She's in the hospital and it doesn't look like she's going to live much longer," said Ferguson Senior.

Fergie told Manager Durocher. Leo told him to get home.

"My mother was in intensive care when I saw her. She was down to sixty or seventy pounds," said Fergie.

She could barely whisper, but she said, "Fergie don't worry, you have your own life to live. I've lived a full life and I am happy. I'm going to see Christ."

Fergie's mother died on September 15, 1970. It was her wedding anniversary. She was only fifty-two years old.

"The main thing I found out about her when she died was that I did not lose a mother — I lost a friend, a counsellor, a teacher, and a person who was there when I needed her," said Fergie.

Fergie had a tattoo on his left arm that read: "Trust in God." He had it done in 1968 when his mother was first diagnosed with cancer. When she died, the tattoo served as a reminder to keep the faith, never give up, and strive harder.

Fergie's dad told him that he should rejoin the Cubs, who were in St. Louis. Fergie called Durocher and told him he would rejoin the team. He felt it would take more courage to pitch than not to pitch. But Leo turned him down.

"No, you stay there," said Durocher. "I want you to be with your family."

At the funeral, both father and son broke down crying. That was hard on Fergie. He had never seen his father cry.

Right after the funeral, Fergie went to Chicago to pick up some clothes. He travelled to Montreal. The next day the Cubs were to open a series against the Montreal Expos.

When Fergie got to Montreal, he told Durocher and Becker that he wanted to pitch that night. He needed only one more win to make it a twenty-win season.

Fergie winds up for a pitch at the height of his career with the Cubs.

Canadian Baseball

The Montreal Expos became Canada's first major-league baseball team in 1969. They never won a World Series. For financial reasons, the team relocated to Washington D.C. before the 2005 season. The Montreal Expos became the Washington Nationals. The Toronto Blue Jays became Canada's second major-league team in 1977. They became known as Canada's team when they won back-to-back World Series championships in 1992 and 1993.

But the start wasn't about that. He wanted to do something to honour his mother's memory. Durocher didn't argue with Fergie's reason.

Fergie pitched his way to his twentieth victory. He knew it was what his mother would have expected of him.

On October 2, the Cubs defeated the New York Mets 4–1, getting them a second-place finish in the final standings. In that game Fergie allowed only two hits. It was his twenty-second victory and twenty-fourth complete game of the season. Fergie's turnaround was one of the main reasons the Cubs finished high in the standings.

Fergie finished the 1970 season with a 22–13 record. It was his fourth twenty-win season in a row. It was beginning to look like a habit.

11 A Canadian First

The pitching mound was Fergie's office at the ballpark. It was where he worked during the game. He had just one thought on his mind when he was throwing from the mound. All he wanted to do was throw strikes.

"Any time Fergie went out to the mound it gave us a lot of confidence that we were going to win the ball game that day," said Cubs outfielder Billy Williams.

Pitching was easy for Fergie once he

found his groove. He used to tease the hitters by throwing inside and outside, up and down. He didn't have the blazing fastball of pitcher Bob Gibson. But Gibson was the pitcher Fergie was usually compared to. This bothered Fergie because they were very different pitchers. Fergie's greatness was a matter of control.

"I had four pitches and I could control them all," said Fergie. He threw a fastball, curveball, slider, and changeup. "I used to get angry when I was compared to Gibson.

Setting Goals

Fergie and Cubs outfielder Billy Williams shared a ritual at the beginning of each season. They would write down their goals for the upcoming season. Fergie would write down how many games he was going to win. They would put their predictions in a sealed envelope that was not opened until the end of the season.

I didn't want to be compared to anybody. I pitched like Fergie Jenkins."

There were days, he remembered, when pitching was like shaking hands with the catcher.

"He'd put the target there and boom, I'd throw it to the target," said Fergie. He felt on those days that he could control everything.

"I maintain he had the best control of any pitcher I played with or against," said Kenny Holtzman, a fellow Cubs pitcher. "If he threw 100 pitches, he could throw between 95 and 100 pitches as strikes. But beyond that, he was durable and dependable. I remember plenty of times when his arm was tired, when he had aches and pains, but he always went out there."

Fergie had missed only two pitching starts in four seasons. He became known for pitching complete games. In his career, he pitched complete games in over half his starts.

"Leo Durocher used to tell me, 'When I send you out there, you're there for the distance, kid.' We never had much of a bullpen in Chicago, but my mother always told me to finish things I started, so I was used to it," said Fergie.

Baseball writers rated the Cubs as one of the prime contenders in the National League race in 1971.

Fergie pitched in the 1971 season opener for the Cubs. He faced the St. Louis Cardinals and their ace pitcher Bob Gibson.

Gibson pitched one of his best games, according to Cubs hitters. But Fergie threw the best game any of the players on either side had seen him pitch. Joe Torre hit a homerun against Fergie to score the only run for the Cardinals. Fergie retired twenty of the last twenty-one hitters. He gave up only three hits and no walks in a 2–1 victory.

Fergie lost the next two starts. Fortunately, he didn't let this continue into a losing skid. He turned his game around and won seven straight games.

During this stretch of victories, Fergie won his ninety-ninth career game. This made him the all-time Canadian winner in major-league history. It put him ahead of Russ Ford of Brandon, Manitoba. It took four more games for Fergie to win his 100th career victory.

By June 10, Fergie had a win–loss record of 10–5. He had pitched twelve complete games. With this record, he was, once again, picked to play in the 1971 All Star Game. In that game he pitched just one inning. It wasn't a very good outing, as he gave up a homerun to Harmon Kilebrew and a single to Brooks Robinson.

By the start of August, Fergie was driving hard to show that he should be considered for the Cy Young Award. He continued to pile up the victories. He was getting close to a fifth straight twenty-win season. Unfortunately, he still had not attracted the attention given to pitchers like Bob Gibson and Juan Marichal.

"He may not have gotten as much publicity as he deserved," said Atlanta Braves Hank Aaron. "But, I don't think there is a hitter in the league that underestimates him."

Fergie's first shot for his twentieth victory came against the Houston Astros on August 20. He got off to a shaky start. Fergie gave up three singles and two runs in the first inning. However, the Cubs looked after him in the next inning by scoring three runs.

"I never even considered taking him out," said Durocher. "There were games I took him out and I wished I hadn't."

Fergie pitched a complete game to a 3–2 victory. He became the first major-league pitcher since Warren Spahn in 1960 and the second Cubs pitcher to record a fifth straight twenty-win season.

The Cubs were eliminated from the pennant race on September 14. They finished the season in third place with seventy-nine victories. Fergie kept on winning throughout September. He finished the season with a 24–13 record. He led the league by pitching thirty complete games. He was second in the league in strikeouts with 263.

"The first year I had won twenty games, in 1967, people thought that because the Cubs scored quite a few runs I was lucky," said Fergie. "The second time I won twenty games they thought it was a fluke. The third time they scoffed that because I got so many starts a season it was only to be expected that I would win twenty games. The fourth year I won twenty games people started to think, 'Well, maybe Jenkins is a good pitcher, but not in a class with the best.' The fifth time I did it, a few people thought, 'Maybe he does belong with Gibson, Seaver and Marichal.'"

A Pitcher's Greatest Honour

Cy Young is considered one of the greatest pitchers of all time. During his twenty-two-year career, from 1890 to 1911, he won 511 games. He still holds the record for most career victories. In 1956, one year after his death, Major League Baseball created an award to honour his memory. The Cy Young Award is given to the pitcher voted most effective in the league. Fergie is not the only Canadian to win the Cy Young Award. Former relief pitcher Eric Gagne of the Los Angeles Dodgers won the award in 2003.

The Baseball Writers' Association voted and named Fergie the 1971 National League Cy Young Award winner. He beat out the Mets' Tom Seaver. He became the first Canadian to win the award for best pitcher.

Cy Young might not have looked like an athlete, but he was baseball's greatest pitcher. His incredible 511 – win record might never be equalled.

He was also the first Chicago Cubs pitcher to win it.

That winter, Fergie looked toward the next season. He wanted to win another twenty games, something every pitcher strives for. But Fergie was looking for more. He knew he was one of the league's top pitchers. He wanted the respect and money that came along with that success.

12 A Class by Himself

Baseball made Fergie happy, but it didn't make him rich. Every year he had a contract battle with the Cubs general manager John Holland. Holland was the person who decided how much the ball club would pay each player.

If Fergie was a pitcher today he would be paid tens of millions of dollars a season. It was very different back then. The players were just as good, but they were paid nowhere near the same amount. In 1971, only a few players made more than $100,000 a season. This included the star players, future Hall of Fame members. Today, the minimum salary is $350,000 a season. Very few players receive that little. But back in 1972, baseball players made just a little above what the average person watching in the stands made.

Before the 1972 season started, Fergie was in a contract battle with Holland. After five twenty-win seasons in a row, he wanted to be paid like one of the top pitchers in the league. With that record he was one, but Cubs management always had excuses why he wasn't paid the same wage. He now had one thing more than another twenty-win season to back up his argument for more money. The Cubs could not refuse the 1971 Cy Young Award winner's request.

When the 1972 season started, Fergie finally became one of the top-paid players in baseball. He signed a two-year contract worth $125,000 a season.

Fergie pitched in his sixth season opener in seven years. He was still the Cubs ace pitcher. For that big contract, the team wanted another great year. Fergie wanted that, too, but something wasn't right. He felt aches and pains he had never felt before.

At the beginning of the season Fergie hurt his knee sliding into home plate. He also felt tightening in his right shoulder and a twitch in his pitching arm.

He lost the first two games of the season. He eventually turned things around and he started to win games. So he didn't tell anybody about his arm trouble.

For the first half of the season he won more than he lost. By early July, he had a 11–8 record, and the Cubs were only three-and-a-half games out of first place. But the Cubs put together a disappointing

July. By July 23 they had dropped to ten games out of first place. They never contended for the pennant for the rest of the season.

During that time, Manager Leo Durocher stepped down from his position. His plan for a World Series championship had not worked out. He was replaced by Whitey Lockman. Fergie pitched the first game after Lockman took over the club. It was one of the best games he ever pitched. He defeated the Phillies 4–0.

After winning his eighteenth game of the season, Fergie talked to George Langford of the *Chicago Tribune*.

"On August 30, I'm going to have a scoop for you writers," said Fergie.

Langford laughed. "What are you going to do, Fergie? Announce your new eight-part peace proposal?"

"No, I'm going to give you a story," Fergie replied. "Just be there when I win my twentieth game. I'm going to set the record straight about myself. I think you'll be interested."

It took until September 8 for Fergie to pitch his twentieth victory. He was eight days off schedule, but he made it.

After the game, the reporters crowded the Cubs locker room in Veterans Stadium in Philadelphia. Fergie didn't wait for them to start asking questions. He started talking.

"What I'm going to say may shock the fans and maybe they won't take it the right way but I'm going to say it anyway," Fergie said. "I no longer want to be categorized with other pitchers. I want people to say that Fergie Jenkins belongs in a class by himself. That's a great class to be in and these great Cubs players — Ron Santo, Billy Williams, Randy Hundley — have put me in the class by scoring runs for the team."

Fergie's six straight twenty-win seasons record equalled Three-Finger Brown, the Chicago Cubs pitcher shown in this baseball card. Brown had only three fingers on his pitching hand.

"I'm not saying that I'm a better pitcher than anyone else, but I have done something that others haven't. Among active pitchers that puts me in a class by myself. Never in my wildest dreams did I think, six years ago, I could win twenty [games] six years in a row. I just hope God keeps me healthy and that I keep going."

There were mixed reactions to his statement. Some people thought he was bragging. Did he think he belonged on a pedestal above everybody else?

"My statement was interpreted as a boast that I thought myself a better pitcher than Juan Marichal, Seaver, and Gibson," said Fergie. "That is not what I was saying. What I meant was that I did not want to be compared with them. I wanted to be evaluated on my own merit. I wanted to be considered as an individual.

"I was praising the Cubs, the players on my team who, with their hitting and fielding, had given me the opportunity to be in a different class than Marichal, Gibson, and Seaver."

For the rest of the season, Fergie's arm and shoulder gave him trouble. Several times he had to leave games in pain during the late innings. Near the end of the season his arm was hurting all the time.

The pain in his arm got so bad that he went to a surgeon. The doctor told him all the arm needed was a long rest. Fergie did not pitch another inning in 1972.

"The future looks good for me and the Cubs. I am not worried a lot about my arm," said Fergie during the winter layoff. "I know that I can continue to win and that the guys on the ball club are going to help me. The best years of the Cubs and Ferguson Jenkins are still to come."

13 Comeback

The 1973 season started out as a good one for the Cubs. By the end of June the club was six-and-a-half games ahead in first place. It again looked as though the Cubs might make it all the way to the pennant.

Fergie started the season with high hopes. But his body wasn't healed. His shoulder was still sore through spring training. The pain was from pitching so many innings for seven straight years. Nothing helped take away the pain. He even tried to change the way he pitched.

Through the pain, Fergie kept pitching well. As he coasted to his sixth win early in the season, he seemed to be on the way to another twenty-win season.

But the Cubs could not keep their first-place position in the standings. The team and Fergie began to lose. Team morale went to an all-time low. Fergie was disappointed with his performance. One of his losing streaks ran for six games. After so much success, everything seemed to be going wrong. The fans booed him, and some even called him a quitter.

"I haven't really felt excited about 1973 and I guess it's showed in my performance this year," said Fergie. "You play a game for a certain amount of time and you enjoy what you're doing, but I haven't enjoyed it in 1973."

There was nothing good to say about the Cubs' 1973 season. They finished second-to-last in their division with a 77–84 record. Fergie finished the season with a 14–16 record. He asked the Cubs to trade him.

"I called Mr. Holland right after our last ball game and told him a change of uniforms would probably do me a lot of good," said Fergie.

Fergie had nothing against the Cubs fans or the team. He just wanted to see if a new team would bring back the magic he'd had for six seasons.

Chicago Cubs owner P. K. Wrigley (of the Wrigley Chewing Gum Company) expressed disgust with his team's performance in 1973. He had several highly-paid players on the roster. He couldn't afford to keep them when they weren't able to produce a pennant.

"Definitely ready for a major overhaul," said Wrigley. "Whitey Lockman can return as manager. I can't say that any of the others earned their money this season."

A Canadian Superstar

Fergie was named the Canadian Press Male Athlete of the Year four times — in 1967, 1968, 1971, and 1972. In 1974 he was awarded the Lou Marsh Trophy as the Canadian Athlete of the Year. He was also given a star on Canada's Walk of Fame.

Fergie always said he would like to be traded to the Montreal Expos. He wanted to play baseball in his home country. The Cubs did not listen because they had other plans.

As far as the Cubs were concerned, Fergie was finished. The Cubs said Fergie was all washed up in the big leagues. He was getting old. He had a bad back and a bad arm.

Fergie was traded to the Texas Rangers in the American League. The thirty-year-old veteran pitcher was traded for the hot young star Bill Madlock. Some fans and sportswriters were surprised that the

Rangers gave up Madlock for the aging Fergie. They thought Texas was making a big mistake.

At the beginning of the 1974 season, baseball writers picked Texas to finish at the bottom of their division. These same writers wrote that Fergie would never win twenty games again.

In 1973, the Texas Rangers had a 57–105 record. With Fergie in 1974, they had a much improved 84–76 record. They finished second in their division, only five games behind the World Series champions, the Oakland A's.

Fergie had the best season of his career. He had a 25–12 record and tied for the league lead in wins. He had an ERA of 2.83, pitched twenty-nine complete games, and struck out 225.

Fergie finished second in the American League Cy Young Award voting, and was fifth for the league MVP. He was named

Major League Baseball's Comeback Player of the Year.

Fergie went on to win seventeen games in 1975. But it wasn't a great season. With eighteen losses and a high 3.93 ERA, Fergie's days as a Ranger were numbered.

"We have some great young pitching prospects. I'd like to give the ball to those young pitchers and let them develop," said Texas Rangers manager Brad Corbett.

"I didn't pitch that well last year and with my high salary I'm usually one of the first to get looked at or asked about by other clubs," said Fergie. "I think I still have a couple of twenty-game seasons left in my arm."

On November 12, 1975, Fergie was traded to the Boston Red Sox of the American League. He admitted he was hurt when Texas traded him during the off-season.

14 Troubled Career

Fergie was looking for another chance to regain his earlier glory. He touched it for one season in 1974, but lost it the next. Maybe in Boston he could turn things around.

Boston was not like Chicago or Texas. The Red Sox were not the "lovable losers" of the American League. Each year they put together a team they thought could win a World Series. Boston was just coming off a World Series appearance in 1975. They were one win away from a title. The team had high expectations for Fergie. They thought he would help them get to another World Series.

The Red Sox started the 1976 season in a big slump. By May 12, they had lost ten straight games and were in last place in their division. Fergie had a 1–5 record. The fans and the management were not pleased with the team. They had expected a winning ball club.

The season eventually turned around for the team and for Fergie. By the beginning of August, the Red Sox were fighting for first place. Fergie had pitched himself to a 11–8 record. But a winning record was still not enough for Boston fans.

Fergie's 1976 season ended when he suffered a torn achilles tendon. He had a 12–11 record. Over the winter Fergie underwent surgery to correct the injury. It took him all off-season to get back into pitching form.

Fergie started the 1977 season strong by winning four games in four starts. At a game against the Chicago White Sox, he passed the record of pitching great Sandy Koufax in career strikeouts. He moved to fourteenth on the all-time strikeout list with 2,397. He was given a standing ovation by the crowd.

Unfortunately, that success would not continue. Over a six-week period, Fergie went without a victory. He was struggling. He blamed his lack of drive for the win drought that had started on June 23. He didn't win another game until August 4.

"In Boston, if you don't pitch well, you don't pitch," said Fergie. "There is no such thing as waiting out a slump."

He was taken out of the starting rotation in September. He was sent to the bullpen and never pitched another inning in 1977.

"I put Jenkins in the bullpen for long

relief but our pitchers have been going past five innings," said Red Sox manager Don Zimmer. "Now he might as well sit on the bench, because we won't be using him."

Because Fergie won just twenty-two games in his two years with the Red Sox, it was assumed by most people that he was washed up. But Fergie didn't think so.

"I feel good, my arm is fine, and I think I can still win with regular work," said Fergie.

But Fergie did realize that he was finished with Boston. On December 14, Fergie was traded back to the Texas Rangers.

"I was kind of surprised at first and then happy because I did perform well the two years I was with them," said Fergie.

It was a different Fergie returning to Texas. He was not seen as the seven-time twenty-game winner anymore. He was the pitcher who had struggled for the past two seasons. Texas didn't see him as a starting pitcher. Instead he was brought back as a relief pitcher.

Texas coach Billy Hunter had his doubts about how Fergie would pitch. Fergie had to change people's minds. Some critics said Fergie was just pitching to claim his salary.

"I'd never just hang around," said Fergie in reply. "I think I can still pitch. I've learned so much in seventeen years.

"I'd like to win 250 games. That's one goal. I'd also like to win 100 games in each league." He added that he would retire after two more seasons.

The Rangers were picked by many to top the American League West division. But Texas had a very bad start to the season with three wins in their first thirteen games. When the Rangers had lost a string of nine games, Billy Hunter turned to his veteran pitcher in the bullpen. Fergie was moved back into the starting rotation. His first start would be against the Kansas City Royals.

Fergie used the same smooth delivery that marked his style during the glory years with the Cubs. He retired the first eighteen batters. They could not get a hit or even a walk against Fergie. They eventually got four hits, but that was not enough to beat the Rangers. Fergie had pitched his team to a 4–1 victory.

"I think I proved tonight I can still pitch," said Fergie after the game.

With one game, Fergie breathed new life into his fading career.

"Jenkins just did a hell of a job and as far as I'm concerned he is still a master craftsman," said Kansas City manager Whitey Herzog.

By June, Fergie was the ace of the Rangers staff. He showed them he was no washed-up pitcher.

Playing in Canada

Fergie always dreamed about playing pro baseball in Canada. But the Montreal Expos and Toronto Blue Jays never showed interest in him. It wouldn't be until he retired that he got his wish. During the 1984 and 1985 seasons, Fergie pitched and played first base for the London Majors, a semi-pro team. He was the Intercounty Baseball League's most popular player during those seasons. Any earnings he made were donated to charity.

"I guess I've proven a lot of people wrong," said Fergie. "I think I'm pitching as well as I did four years ago."

15 Guilty?

Fergie finished the 1978 season with an 18–8 record. He continued this success into the 1979 season with a 16–14 record.

Before the start of the 1980 season, Fergie had one goal. He was shooting for 250 career wins. It was a goal that could be reached. And just a little more than a month into the season he achieved it. His career was celebrated in newspapers across Canada. He was made a member of the Order of Canada. This is one of the highest honours given to a Canadian citizen.

In August, Fergie hit the headlines again, but not because of his pitching.

The Rangers had flown from Milwaukee to Toronto on a chartered plane. Four bags failed to go with them. One of those bags belonged to Fergie.

The bags didn't show up the next day or evening. A day after that, a phone call to the hotel advised him that the luggage had been found. However, under Canadian law, the bags would have to be opened because the owner wasn't present. Permission was given to have them checked. When Fergie reached the ballpark, he was arrested. The police had found a small amount of illegal drugs in his bag.

"Right now I'm embarrassed," said Fergie. "All of a sudden, I'm Mr. Bad Guy."

Fergie told Mike Bennett of the Chatham *Daily News* that he felt he had let a lot of people down. This included the team, his friends, and his country.

The person who felt most hurt was the one Fergie had least wanted to hurt, his father. Ferguson Senior had always regarded his son as a hero, and this was a blow to him. It was about two years before he believed Fergie didn't do it.

"I was stunned by the situation. I did not put drugs in my suitcase and did not know what was going on," said Fergie. "I have contended that I was set up for the arrest and that I have committed no crime."

Five days after he was arrested, Fergie was called into Baseball Commissioner Bowie Kuhn's office. On the advice of his lawyer, Fergie declined to answer questions related to the incident. He didn't want to hurt his position with Canadian authorities.

Fergie was suspended for the rest of the season by the Commissioner. It was because he refused to cooperate with the investigation. Kuhn was handing out a punishment before any wrongdoing had been determined in court.

The Major League Players Association (MLPA) filed a grievance, demanding Fergie be returned to the active roster.

"The association believes Kuhn should not have the power to act against a player when he's yet to be found guilty in a court of law," wrote the *Toronto Star*.

The MLPA won their case against Kuhn. Fergie was reinstated and finished the season with a 12–12 record.

Fergie was tried on December 18, 1980. If he was found guilty at the trial, it would end his baseball career.

"At the time I was scared that my entire life would be ruined and my reputation would be smeared," said Fergie.

In the courtroom, Fergie stood quietly as the judge stated, "You seem to be a person who has conducted himself in exemplary fashion in the community and in the country building up an account. This is the time to draw on that account."

He was found guilty of illegal drug possession. But the verdict was later erased and he was freed without penalty. The effect was the same as if he had not been convicted.

Even though he was said to be not guilty, public opinion still said he was guilty. The drug charges would not leave him for the rest of his career. Some people heard only part of the story and thought he was a drug addict.

"Those who followed the case realized I was not a criminal, but even now some people just immediately react when they hear my name and blame me for being involved with drugs," said Fergie.

This all kept Fergie's mind off baseball during the 1981 season. He posted a 5–8 record.

Banned

Major League Baseball has a long list of drugs that players are banned from taking. They cannot use, possess, or sell them. This list is divided into three categories: drugs of abuse, steroids, and stimulants. Drugs of abuse are illegal drugs like cocaine or heroin. Steroids and stimulants are performance-enhancing drugs.

At the end of the 1981 season, he was released by the Rangers. He became a free agent and could sign with any team. But he had to find a team that wanted to sign him. He would have to retire if no team stepped up to say they wanted him. It looked like that might happen.

16 One Last Chance

Not many teams showed much interest in Fergie. Most thought his career as a major-league pitcher was over. The team that showed the most interest was familiar to him. The Chicago Cubs had given him a chance as a young player to pitch in the major leagues. They were ready to do it again now with the thirty-eight-year-old veteran. On December 8, 1981, Fergie signed with the Cubs.

The Cubs were a last place team in

1981. They brought in Manager Dallas Green to change things. Green had managed the Phillies to a World Series championship in 1980. The Cubs were hoping that magic would rub off on his new team. He brought many of his players with him from Philly. He was excited to also have Fergie.

"I know he can pitch and he's a good competitor," said Green. "We have a fairly young staff and we feel he will give us some stability to go with them. Fergie is going after 3,000 strikeouts and I'm gambling those kinds of goals will make him rise to the occasion."

By this time, Fergie was the winner of 264 major-league games. People thought he might make the Hall of Fame someday. But after a poor 1981 season, he was just hanging on to his major-league career.

Fergie was positive about getting the Cubs out of last place.

"I feel this is the year they can shake that attitude of being losers. I just hope I'm one of the players that help them do it," said Fergie. "I really want to make this deal look good. Dallas went out on a limb for me and I appreciate that."

The Chicago media didn't have high hopes for the Cubs in 1982.

"At present, Cubs pitching strikes fear in the hearts of only their fans. The staff is sprinkled with boys who have never won and men who hope to win again," stated the *Chicago Tribune*.

Fergie pitched the home opening game on April 9 in Chicago. The game was played in near-freezing weather. The ground crew spent the morning clearing the field of snow.

Fergie pitched a great game for the Cubs. He was relieved late in the game. Fans, bundled up in overcoats and windbreakers, gave Fergie a loud cheer.

Across the headlines of the *Chicago Tribune* Sports Section it read: "Old Fergie Good As New." The Cubs won the game 5–0. Fergie got credit for the victory.

Fergie became the seventh major-league pitcher to get 3,000 strikeouts. It was for a game in San Diego against the Padres. They stopped the game as the crowd gave Fergie a two-minute standing ovation.

By June 5, he had only a 3–7 record. The Cubs were not doing very well either. But the team and Fergie would eventually put some wins together. He would end the season with a 14–15 record. Surprisingly, he was the pitcher with the most wins on the Cubs pitching staff.

After the 1982 season, Fergie signed a two-year contract. He was not ready to retire. He now had two goals to fulfill in his career. He wanted to record 300 wins, and he wanted to win a World Series.

"When I was younger I never thought as far ahead as to have a goal of winning 300 games," said Fergie. "When I got 250 wins, I started to think that maybe I had a chance to do it."

Fergie didn't feel the pressure to prove himself in the spring of 1983 that he had felt the year before. The 1983 season started off well for Fergie. By June 5 he had a record of 3–3. But then he had eleven straight starts without a win. When his record dropped to 5–9 on September 4, he was taken out of the starting rotation. He was sent to the bullpen for the rest of the season.

"He wore his proud face after being relocated to the bullpen a few weeks ago and he was deeply hurt by the move," wrote the *Chicago Tribune*.

Fergie did not want to be remembered for a 6–9 record. But he said, "I was going to quit three years ago after 250 wins, so these are the gravy years."

Near the end of his career, Fergie spent more time on the bench than he did pitching.

Even with a contract, Fergie was not sure if he fit into the Chicago Cubs' plans for 1984. By the end of spring training he was cut loose by the team.

Fergie thought he still could pitch, but said, "I was the oldest pitcher on the team at forty-one and they were looking for younger talent." He lacked only sixteen victories to reach the 300-win mark.

"Other teams phoned but I didn't want to win with another team. I didn't want to be a countdown player. If I was going to win 300, I wanted to do it with the Cubs," said Fergie. "I played twenty-two years and it's been a lot of fun. But there's a time and a place to say, 'Hey, it's all done.'"

Fergie always felt that if he was given the chance, he could have won the sixteen

Life After Baseball

Fergie never fully left baseball after retiring as a player. He was a minor-league pitching coach in the Texas Rangers organization. He was the Chicago Cubs pitching coach during the 1995 and 1996 seasons. Off the field, Fergie had always helped raise money for charities. In 2000 he founded the Fergie Jenkins Foundation. He now uses his time to raise money for the charities his foundation supports.

games that would have made him a 300-game winner. That would have made him a lock for the Baseball Hall of Fame. But he had already done enough. He ended his career with a 284–226 record. He had 3,192 strikeouts and only 997 walks. He is the only pitcher in history to have 3,000 strikeouts and fewer than 1,000 walks. He finished eleventh on the all-time strikeout list.

He would now have to wait to see if he would become a member of the Baseball Hall of Fame.

Epilogue

Fergie was inducted into the US Baseball Hall of Fame on July 21, 1991. A total of 443 members of the Baseball Writers' Association of America cast votes that year. Fergie received 334 votes, making the cut by one vote to became the first Canadian elected to the Baseball Hall of Fame.

Baseball might be America's game, but on that day a maple leaf was placed in the middle of it. A dozen busloads of people came from Chatham to support one of their hometown heroes. Sitting : the proud Chatham citizens were other Canadians who wanted to watch one of their own get his due.

"This is Canada's finest hour," said George Knee of Toronto. "I thought it was important for us to come down here and pay a little respect to Canada's greatest ballplayer."

Sitting front and centre was Ferguson Jenkins, Senior.

"This is not the kind of thing that happens every day to a Canadian, is it? If Fergie's mother was here today she'd be floating on air," said Fergie's father. "I never thought I would live to see this day."

As Fergie stepped out onto the podium to accept his plaque, the Chatham Concert Band played the song "Canadian Sunset." It was the tune often played when Fergie stepped up to bat.

Fergie thanked cities, countries, fans,

high-school teachers, family, and managers in his acceptance speech. He also thanked the two most important people in his life.

"This day is also for my father," Fergie said. "He was my first teacher. He inspired me. He was a great outfielder. He was known as Hershey. It was my father who taught me to be kind, conscientious, and responsible. It was my father who instilled the love of baseball in me. This day I am not being inducted alone. I am being inducted on July 21, 1991, with my father Ferguson Jenkins, Sr."

"Mother," said Jenkins, who paused before he could continue, "knew before I did that the sport of baseball is what I should play. Although she never saw me play, she knew. Thank you, mother."

Fergie had received many honours in Canada and the United States. Over the years he was named to many different Halls of Fame. He is a member of the

Canadian Baseball, Ontario Sports, Chicago Cubs, Texas Rangers, Chatham Sports, and Canadian Sports Halls of Fame. In 2009 the Cubs retired his number '31' at a ceremony at Wrigley Field.

They recognized his career as a major-league ballplayer. Above and beyond all that, he would be known as the man who was once a boy in Chatham, Ontario. He would be remembered as the man whose hard work and determination took him to the highest level in the game he loved.

Glossary

Ace: A team's best starting pitcher.

Ball: A pitch that is not thrown in the strike zone or swung at by the batter.

Bases loaded: When there is a runner on each base.

Base on balls/Walk: To allow a batter to reach first base by pitching four balls.

Box score: A statistical summary of a baseball game. It shows if a player got a hit, run, or was substituted during a game.

Bullpen: The area where relief pitchers warm-up before entering a game.

Changeup: A slow pitch that is meant to look much faster.

Clutch situation: When a big hit or strikeout could determine the outcome of a game.

Complete game: The record given to a starting pitcher for pitching an entire game without being replaced by a relief pitcher.

Control pitcher: A pitcher who succeeds mostly by using accurate pitches to get batters out. Power pitchers rely on velocity.

Curve ball: A pitch that curves after it is thrown.

Earned run: A run scored on a hit, walk, or steal.

Earned run average (ERA): A statistic that shows the number of earned runs allowed per nine innings pitched. The lower the ERA the better.

Error: A defensive mistake that allows a batter to stay at the plate, reach first base, or advance a base runner.

Extra innings: When a game is tied after nine innings, more innings are played until one team scores more runs than the other.

Fastball: A straight, hard pitch.

Hit: A play in which the batter safely reaches a base after hitting the ball.

Homerun: A fair ball hit out of the playing field.

Inning: A period of play. There are nine innings in a baseball game. Each team bats in an inning until they reach three outs.

Line up: A team's batting order and fielding position.

Mound: The hill the pitcher stands on while pitching.

Pennant: A banner or flag that the winning team is awarded to display in their ballpark to show they won a championship.

Pennant race: Teams competing for a league championship. The winner is awarded the pennant.

Pitch: The act of throwing a baseball toward home plate.

Pitching rotation: The order in which starting pitchers take turns starting games. They usually have three or four days rest between starts.

Relief pitcher: The pitcher replacing the starting pitcher.

Slider: A pitch that appears to be a fastball until it reaches home plate, then it curves quickly to confuse the batter.

Strike: A strike is called if a batter swings at a pitch and misses or if the pitch passes through the strike zone.

Strike zone: The area over home plate between the batter's armpits and knees. Any pitch thrown through this area is called a strike.

World Series: A best of seven-game series played between the champions of the American and National Leagues.

Acknowledgements

This book was researched using many different primary resources. I looked through various newspaper archives when learning about Fergie's career. These newspaper archives include the *New York Times*, *Toronto Star*, *Globe and Mail*, and the *Chicago Tribune*.

Many of my past Recordbooks were about subjects that had never been written about before. So I really had to dig deep to find those stories. With Fergie Jenkins I had many secondary resources. These were either books written by Fergie or books by other authors about his career. These sources let me go deeper into the life of Fergie off and on the field.

The books I used included Fergie's two autobiographies: *Fergie — My life from the Cubs to Cooperstown*, published in 2009, and *Like Nobody Else: The Ferguson Jenkins story*, published in 1973. Another book I used was *The Game is Easy, Life is Hard: The story of Ferguson Jenkins* written by Dorothy Turcotte and published in 2002. I also found a children's book published in 1975 called *Ferguson Jenkins: The quiet winner*. It was written by Stanley Pashko.

I would like to acknowledge the help given to me by the Fergie Jenkins Foundation. Through the process of writing this book I decided to pledge a percentage of my royalties from the sale of this book to the Foundation.

Lastly, I would like to thank my understanding editors at James Lorimer & Company and my understanding wife at home, Shelley. They all played an important role in my researching and writing of this book.

About the Author

Richard Brignall is a journalist from Kenora, Ontario. He has written articles for *Cottage Life* and *Outdoor Canada*. He was previously a sports reporter for the *Kenora Daily Miner and News*. He is the author of several books in the Recordbooks series.

Photo Credits

Courtesy of the Fergie Jenkins
   Foundation: p. 17, p. 135
Library of Congress, Prints &
   Photographs Division: pp. 18–19 (LC–
   USZ62–132218), p. 43 (LC–DIG–fsa–
   8a03228), p. 48 (LC–DIG–ppmsca–
   03128), pp. 70–71 (LC–USZ62–111825),
   p. 101 (LC–USZ62–77897), p. 108 (LC–
   DIG–bbc–1654f)
Archives of Ontario: p. 23 (Department
   of Travel and Publicity, Publicity
   Branch, Street scene, Chatham, 1960,
   RG 65–35–3, 11764–X4237)
National Baseball Hall of Fame Library,
   Cooperstown, NY: cover, p. 24, p. 90

Index

A

All Star appearance, 80-81, 97
Allen, Doug, 29, 30
Allen, Richie, 52, 54
Arkansas Travelers, 50, 56
awards (*see also* Cy Young Award), 80, 81, 82, 97, 101–102, 115, 124, 137, 140-1

B

Baltimore Orioles, 11
Baseball Hall of Fame, *see* Hall of Fame
Baseball Writers' Association of America, 10, 11, 101, 138
basketball career, 83
Becker, Joe (coach), 86, 87, 90
Bell, Cool Papa, 20
Bench, Johnny, 10
Bunning, Jim, 35, 60-1

C

career, first contract, 37
   first games, 46, 60
Chatham Junior Baseball, 29
Chatham Maroons, 24
Chattanooga Lookouts, 55
childhood, 14-15, 21
colour barrier, 18, 19, 20
   hockey, 22
Cooperstown, (*see also* Hall of Fame), 9, 146
Cundle, Mark, 29
Cy Young Award, 82, 98, 100, 101, 104, 115

D

Doby, Larry, 25, 26
Durocher, Leo (manager), 67, 68, 71, 72, 73, 74, 76, 77, 78, 88, 89, 90, 91, 96, 98, 106
Dzadura, Gene, 33, 34, 37

F

farm system (*see* minor leagues)
Ferguson Jenkins Day, 75

G

Gibson, Josh, 20
Green, Dallas (manager), 131, 132

H

Hall of Fame, 9, 11, 104, 131, 137
   elected to, 10, 138-140
   eligibility, 9
   nominations, 10
Hilldale Baseball team, 18
Holland, John, 103, 104, 113
Howe, Jack, 29

K

Kansas City Monarchs, 18, 20

L

Lang, Jack, 11
Lopez, Marcelino, 54
Lucadello, Tony, 36, 37
Lucchesi, Frank, 44

M

Mauch, Gene (manager), 59, 60, 61, 64, 65
McLish, Cal (coach), 60
Miami Marlins, 45, 49, 54
minor leagues, 40, 55
Montreal Royals, 20
Morgan, Joe, 11

N

Negro Leagues, 15, 20, 53
Negro Leagues, World Series, 18

O

O'Ree, Willie, 22, 23, 25

P

Paige, Satchel, 20
Palmer, Jim, 11
Phillips, Adolfo, 64, 67
prejudice, 42, 43, 46–56

R

records, (*see* awards)
retirement, 10
Robinson, Jackie, (*see also* colour barrier) 19, 20, 24, 53
rookie card, 65

S

salary, 37, 50, 103–4, 105
segregation (prejudice)
Seminuk, Paul (manager), 49, 59
statistics, 50, 54, 55, 60, 63, 69, 81, 82, 87, 92, 95, 96, 97, 99, 115, 118, 119, 124, 127, 129, 131, 133, 134, 137

U

Underground Railroad, 16

W

World Series, 70, 76, 91, 106, 115, 117, 131, 133
Wrigley Field, 70, 141

Y

Yastrzemski, Carl 10

More gripping underdog tales of sheer determination and talent!

◎ RECORDBOOKS

Recordbooks are action-packed true stories of Canadian athletes who have changed the face of sport. Check out these titles available at bookstores or your local library, or order them online at www.lorimer.ca.

Big Train: The legendary ironman of sport, Lionel Conacher
   by Richard Brignall
Choice of Colours: The pioneering African-American quarterbacks who changed the face of football by John Danakas
Crazy Canucks: The uphill battle of Canada's downhill ski team
   by Eric Zweig
Fearless: The story of George Chuvalo, Canada's greatest boxer
   by Richard Brignall
Fighting for Gold: The story of Canada's sledge hockey Paralympic gold
   by Lorna Schultz Nicholson
Fire on the Water: The red-hot career of superstar rower Ned Hanlan
   by Wendy A. Lewis
Forever Champions: The enduring legacy of the record-setting Edmonton Grads by Richard Brignall
Knockout!: How "Little Giant" Tommy Burns became the World Heavyweight Champion by Rebecca Sjonger
Lacrosse Warrior: The life of Mohawk lacrosse champion Gaylord Powless
   by Wendy A. Lewis
Long Shot: How the Winnipeg Falcons won the first Olympic hockey gold
   by Eric Zweig
Pink Power: The first Women's World Hockey Champions
   by Lorna Schultz Nicholson
Small Town Glory: The story of the Kenora Thistles' remarkable quest for the Stanley Cup by John Danakas and Richard Brignall
Star Power: The legend and lore of Cyclone Taylor
   by Eric Zweig
Tough Guys: Hockey rivals in times of war and disaster
   by Eric Zweig